learning to serve serving to learn

student book

learning to serve serving to learn

a christian service program for students

joseph moore

AVE MARIA PRESS Notre Dame, Indiana 46556

International Standard Book Number: 0-87793-526-2

Library of Congress Catalog Card Number: 94-70327

Book design and illustration by Elizabeth J. French

Photography:

Frank Casella 11; Cleo Freelance Photo 30, 71, 86; Rev. Patrick Delahanty 15 (bottom); Dale D. Gehman 90; Roger W. Neal 36; Marilyn Nolt 79; Carl Rogers Photography 82; James L. Shaffer cover, 42, 47, 54, 60, 79; Steve and Mary Skjold 16, 24, 27, 66, 79; Jim Whitmer 48, 80, 88, 106.

Printed and bound in the United States of America.

Contents

Part 2: Appendix

introduction

Beginnings

The one thing John and Linda seemed to have in common was that they were both able to fasten their seat belts. Other than that, the two fifteen-year-olds were a marked contrast sitting in the back seat of the four-door sedan.

Linda crossed her legs. And then recrossed them. She flipped the lid on the armrest's ashtray in time with the easy-listening music that played on the radio. She strained her head from side to side to make sure that none of her friends were watching.

Meanwhile John rested his head on the soft pad behind his seat. He took one or two calm glances toward the front dashboard and the digital clock. His turn was coming next. Really, he couldn't wait to begin. This was the first day of driver's training.

New experiences may be scary, exhilarating, challenging, and difficult all at once. Your participation in this Christian service program may awaken some of these same feelings. Why? Christian service is an adult calling, one fraught with new tasks and responsibilities. To do well in the program will require not only your full effort, but your full effort doing some things you may have never tried before.

This book is meant to explain some of the new things to you. Its purpose is to define the people, experiences, assignments, and objectives of the program. It will also help to provide a routine and schedule that you are used to; used with others this book works very well with a class in school or a youth group or confirmation class in a parish.

What's in the Book

Your teacher, youth minister, confirmation coordinator, or other adult leader takes on a new title in this book: *service program director*. The new title describes very well what this person will do. He or she will be your connection with your starting point (school or parish). He or she may recommend or assign your service project. He or she may tell you the amount of time that you have to complete your work. The service program director will help you to evaluate how you are doing.

Hopefully, you will also have a *service site supervisor* at the place where you do your service. If you volunteer at a children's wing of the hospital, your service site supervisor might be one of the nurses on staff. This person is important to you because it is he or she you must contact in order to get the job. While you won't be paid for your service, arranging a volunteer position *is* very much like going on a job interview. You will need to express your talents and skills to the service site supervisor. You will need to tell the service site supervisor about your project and your schedule. Your service site supervisor will also help to evaluate your work in the program.

If you are doing this with a class or parish group, it too may take on a new name and function. Called a *peer support group*, you will meet regularly with other people your own age who are doing service. Though your actual projects will differ, you will find that your experiences—both positive and negative ones—will often be similar. At these meetings, you will discuss your project, share your feelings, pray together, and support each other. Part of your discussion will be on the *essays* and *follow-up activities* that you read and complete from this book.

Two other components of this program go together: *prayer* and *journal writing.* You will be asked to keep a journal, recording the things that happen to you while you serve others and the things you reflect on while you are there and after you leave. Many of your entries will in fact be prayers. A place for you to write your journal entries is included in the appendix of this book. Communicating with God about your work is what helps to define this particular kind of service.

Called to Serve

In the beginning, the scary part of service is just getting started. Deciding what you can do and how you can do it can be difficult. But, like John and Linda were with driver's training, you are obviously poised and ready to begin or you would not be in this program.

Mother Teresa of Calcutta is a modern model of Christian service. Her Missionaries of Charity have taken on the mission of service to the "poorest of the poor." Mother Teresa is often approached with the question, "What can I do to help?" Her advice is always the same.

"Just begin, one, one, one," she says. "Begin at home by saying something good to someone in your family. Begin by helping someone in need in your community, at work, or at school. Begin by making whatever you do something beautiful for God."

Begin.

essays and activities

why service?

OBJECTIVES:

- To determine your motivation in beginning a Christian service program
- To recognize Jesus as the model of servant ministry
- To understand how your spirit and attitude are important parts of your service actions

s you begin a program of Christian service, you probably have many questions. You might wonder, "What can I really do?" Or, "Where is a place that will have me?" Your questions may be even more basic: "How will I get there?" and "When do I have to have this project completed?"

These questions are all important and will be addressed as you share the essays in this text. However, when beginning, the most important question to ask yourself is "Why am I doing this?" As experience has taught you, motivation means everything in doing a task well or poorly. Participating in Christian service is much like taking a course in school, being on a team, or auditioning for a play. Your attitude has a great deal to do with your performance. So, addressing the question—"Why am I doing this?"—which of these responses most closely approximates how you feel?

- I am participating because it's required of me.
- I am participating because I care about the world and the people in it.
- I am participating because when I help others I feel good.
- I am participating because God expects this of me.
- I am participating because I need to list a service component on my college application.

Of course, most people don't do something for one motive alone. But if you truly want to discover a basis for service that will sustain you longer than any other (even beyond the duration of this program), then it is best to look to Jesus as the answer to the question about motivation. For Christians, the love of God translates to love of neighbor. Jesus spoke of this need often. He said:

> "This is my commandment: love one another as I love you. No one has greater love than this, to lay down one's life for one's friends" (Jn 15:12-13).

This "laying down of one's life" is something that Jesus modeled right up until the time of his death on the cross. His ministry was a ministry of service. One of the titles for Jesus is Suffering Servant. In fact, *diakonia,* the Greek word for ministry means "serving like a slave at a table."

At the Last Supper, Jesus got down on his hands and knees and washed the feet of his disciples. Washing another's feet was a common practice in Jesus' time. When guests came to someone's house for dinner, it was customary for their feet to be washed since they had traveled on a dusty or muddy road in sandals. But this task was reserved for servants or slaves. Is it any wonder that the disciples protested when Jesus insisted on doing this himself? Do you remember what Jesus said?

> "If I, therefore, the master and teacher, have washed your feet, you ought to wash another's feet. I have given you a model to follow, so that as I have done for you, you should also do" (Jn 13:15).

Whatever your current motivation, if you are participating in a Christian service program, you will be ministering as Jesus did. This "servant ministry" is one that has no place for people with superior attitudes. Involvement in Christian service sets you apart as a disciple of Jesus, but it doesn't mean that your rewards (for example, feeling good, receiving praise, getting a good grade) should be your ultimate goals. These components are certainly a part of service, just not the main part!

When you get applauded or rewarded for your service, recall Jesus washing the feet of his friends. Root your service in this humility. Remember that even though it is you who serves, you are no better or worse than those who receive your efforts. You too have needs; it just so happens that in this instance you are the one giving rather than receiving.

The Ministry Is the Minister

Another way to look at Jesus' role-modeling is by the phrase "the ministry is the minister." What do you think this means? Another way to put it is that while service involves actions, the spirit and attitude you bring to your actions are equally important. How was this true in Jesus' life?

Spirit and attitude are certainly something to think about as you begin this program. Most anyone can complete the *actions* of Christian service when asked, but can you also bring the right spirit? For example, if a person passes out food to the needy, but is very condescending and rude to the people he or she serves, then he or she is not really being a minister. Or, if someone sits patiently with the elderly and listens to their stories, and yet makes fun of them behind their back, he or she is not doing ministry.

Ministry is a posture toward others, an attitude of openness and caring. It is an attitude that communicates: "I am here for you. For this time and moment, I take on your needs and concerns. Let me be your helper."

So what does all this mean to you? It is impossible for any words, encouragements, teachings, or lessons to change your motivation and attitude about Christian service. This may remain for you a project that "you have to do" or "you need to do." But, as you begin, at least be open to the possibility of something more. The people that you are bound to meet and the work you are to do likely has great meaning. Take some time to examine this service and yourself in new ways.

activity 1-A

a service parable

A lawyer debated Jesus about what he needed to do to inherit eternal life. Jesus told him:

> "You shall love the Lord, your God, with all your heart, with all your being, with all your strength, and with all your mind, and your neighbor as yourself" (Lk 10:27).

The man then asked, "And who is my neighbor?"

To respond, Jesus shared the parable of the Good Samaritan. Read the parable in Luke 10:25-36. It's important to know that Samaritans and Jews were enemies in Jesus' day. Then answer the following questions.

How does the parable illustrate . . .

1. . . . that having a certain role in the church or society doesn't *guarantee* an attitude of service?

2. . . . that the ministry *is* the minister?

3. . . . that service might require putting aside your own plans?

4. . . . that victims often make the best servants?

5. . . . that gratitude is sometimes missing when you serve?

6. . . . that spirit and attitude are an important part of service?

activity 1-B

servant leaders

People who exercise servant leadership often become famous; Martin Luther King, Jr. and Mother Teresa are two recent examples. But there are many more "servant leaders" who are not singled out. Who are the servant leaders you recognize in your own life and experience? Answer the questions that follow.

1. Who are three people you recognize as servant leaders (i.e., a family member, someone you know, a person in the news)?

2. What are two common qualities that each of these people possess?

3. How have they placed the needs of others above their own needs?

4. Choose one of the leaders you listed. What is it that you respect most about this person? How does this person model the servant leadership of Jesus Christ?

putting your gifts to use

OBJECTIVES:

- To appreciate your fundamental goodness
- To examine your personal talents and how they might be used in service of others
- To see how the seven gifts of the Holy Spirit can be of help to you
- To recall that the Spirit is Jesus' gift to you

hat would you find easier to do, make a list of your strengths or a list of your weaknesses? Which list would be longer? Your answers to these questions might reveal a lot about how you feel about yourself.

Usually, a person who thinks more of his or her weaknesses has a low self-esteem or sense of worth. He or she may mask this low self-esteem using a number of different techniques. For example, a girl feels bad because she perceives herself as the only person in the junior class who has never been on a date. Since she does know that she is intellectually bright, she hides her hurt by taking on the role of the class brain and putting down people who are less intelligent. Similarly, a senior football player has low self-esteem, but for an opposite reason. He perceives himself as lacking in academics, so he accents his role as "superjock" and teases others who aren't as physically strong or athletic. These examples of insecurity represent an ailment that many people—young and old—possess. What about you? Do you consider yourself worthwhile for who you are, or because of a particular talent that you have?

Hopefully, you have come to realize that the first and best gift or talent that you have **is** you. You were made in the image of a good and loving Creator God. This fact alone is enough for any positive sense of self worth. Yet, *in addition* to your existence, you were blessed with unique and special gifts. These gifts are not meant to compensate for anything you feel is lacking in your life, but rather are to be celebrated because they *add* to your already good self.

Academics, athletics, music, art, and mechanics are among the variety of gifts that people your age excel at. As you consider a service project, think about your own gifts of this type. Are there any ways that you could combine something that you are good at with your service to others?

St. Paul wrote: "There are different kinds of spiritual gifts but the same Spirit; there are different forms of service but the same Lord" (1 Corinthians 12:4-5). These words tell us that there is nothing better or worse about being the class brain than there is at being the star athlete. What does matter is the effort a person makes in cultivating his or her gifts. And, the attitude he or she takes as the gifts are shared with others.

Gifts of the Spirit

The Holy Spirit offers you many gifts to help you go about the tasks of day-to-day living. Traditionally, they are the gifts of *wisdom, understanding, knowledge, right judgment (counsel), reverence (piety), courage (fortitude),* and *wonder and awe (fear of the Lord).* These gifts are to be used to enhance yourself, to make you the person God intends you to be. These gifts are also to be used for the benefit of others. In the sharing of the gifts of the Spirit, you and those around you are able to glimpse the very life of God.

Examine each of these gifts of the Holy Spirit. Think about how you model these gifts in your life.

1. **Wisdom.** The gift of wisdom goes beyond being "smart." Wisdom allows a person to see the "big picture," how all of life is interrelated, as well as the short-term consequences of things and events. Wisdom involves learning from mistakes and from accumulated life experience.

2. **Understanding.** This gift involves being able to see life from another's perspective, "to walk in another's shoes." Understanding goes hand-in-hand with unselfishness. You need to put aside your own wants and desires in order to be able to listen and respond to the needs of another.

3. **Knowledge.** Are you familiar with the slang phrase "street smarts"? This refers to a type of knowledge that extends out of the intellectual realm and into personal experience. The gift of knowledge is a good teacher. It can help you to learn from all past experiences—good and bad—as you apply them to experiences still to come.

4. **Right Judgment.** "Openness" is another way to describe the gift of right judgment. Right judgment means stepping back from a situation to be able to examine a new direction that is often close at hand. This gift helps you to offer support, suggestions, and encouragement to others.

5. **Reverence.** Reverence means "holiness." Being holy does not have to be an abnormal thing. Utilizing the gift of reverence simply means that you are able to turn to God in prayer and the sacraments for the strength to live a good life.

6. **Courage.** Life has many challenges and setbacks, but a person with courage continues to persevere. This gift helps you to stick with endeavors, tasks, challenges, or relationships that you might otherwise easily give up on.

7. **Wonder and Awe.** Wonder and awe help you to remember that God is Creator and you are created. It helps you to make decisions based on God's way as revealed through the scriptures, the life of Jesus, and the teachings of the church.

These gifts of the Holy Spirit can help you as you consider the direction for your Christian service. Address the Holy Spirit in prayer and ask to be strengthened in these gifts. In addition, as you participate in this ministry, be aware of how these gifts come alive in your words and actions. The Holy Spirit is Jesus' gift to the church (see Jn 14:15-17) and is a gift that is not meant to be hidden. Call on the Spirit to help you be the best you can be and do the best you can do.

activity 2-A

person profiles

Employment agencies often use personality and skill surveys to help determine the right job for applicants. Use this same principle to help you find out how your personal gifts and talents might assist you in your Christian service project. Fill out this survey. Share your responses with two or three others in a small group. Brainstorm with each other on possible service possibilities based on each person's gifts.

A Survey of My Gifts and Talents

1. List at least three gifts, personality traits, or good qualities you possess (example: compassion, good listener, etc.).

2. Share a compliment that others often give you.

3. What is one of your personal gifts that others in your family also share?

4. List at least three ways one or more of your gifts might be used in service to others.

5. List your favorite hobby or extracurricular activity.

6. What is your best talent (academic or non-academic)?

7. How do you work at improving this talent?

8. List at least three ways your best talent might be used in service to others.

activity 2-B

seven gifts

Review the descriptions of the seven gifts of the Holy Spirit from essay 2. On *line 1,* summarize the meaning of each gift in your own words. On *line 2,* write how you can model each gift in your life. Be specific. Discuss both kinds of responses with a partner.

Wisdom

1. ____

2. ____

Understanding

1. ____

2. ____

Knowledge

1. ____

2. ____

Right Judgment

1. ______________________________

2. ______________________________

Reverence

1. ______________________________

2. ______________________________

Courage

1. ______________________________

2. ______________________________

Wonder and Awe

1. ______________________________

2. ______________________________

Jesus said:

> "If you love me, you will keep my commandments. And I will ask the Father and he will give you another Advocate to be with you always, the Spirit of truth, which the world cannot accept, because it neither sees nor knows it. But you know it, because it remains with you, and will be in you" (Jn 14: 15-17).

Finish this prayer. Pray it by yourself or with others.

Dear Holy Spirit, shower me with your gifts. Help me in this time of Christian service . . .

. . . Amen.

choosing a service site

OBJECTIVES:

- To consider two approaches for selecting a service site
- To suggest ways to contact agencies and set up interviews
- To offer several interviewing techniques
- To appreciate your uniqueness

There are generally two ways to go about "choosing a site" for your Christian service. Both involve looking at your talents, gifts, and interests. Also, no matter *how* you go about choosing a site, you can expect the process to entail a fair amount of leg work, that is, effort on your part in order to arrange the relationship between you and the service site supervisor.

The first way to find your service niche is to follow your natural inclinations. For example, a person who has a close relationship with an ailing grandparent may feel drawn to work with other elderly people in a nursing home. Or, someone who is enraged by all the waste encountered in the mountains or the forest while on a hike, may feel naturally drawn to serving an environmental cause. A community organization dedicated to improving the natural environment might be a place to turn.

The second way to go about selecting a service site is just the opposite. Rather than choosing something you are *inclined* to do, you select one that wouldn't normally match with your lifestyle and interests. A shy person might pick a parish ministry like lectoring as a way to get over his or her fear of public speaking. Someone who has never been able to act naturally around mentally retarded people may choose to volunteer some time with the Special Olympics. In this method of selecting, you decide you want to face a new challenge and have new experiences even though you have no known talents that you are aware of for this new task.

Both of these ways of choosing—either based on your natural talents or on your willingness to try something new—are perfectly acceptable. One is not better than the other, just different.

In either case, a good place to begin is to look at some of the practical considerations. What are the opportunities for service in your local parish, neighborhood, or community? Which opportunities offer a schedule that is flexible enough to not conflict with your job, school work, and other extracurricular activities? Also, what are some possible service projects and sites that have been suggested to you by your service program director?

Contacting an Agency

Once you have decided where your interests in ministry are directing you, you need to match those interests with individuals, groups, or agencies that have openings for volunteers. You may be provided with options by your service program director or you may have to seek out service sites yourself. If you are contacting an agency, ordinarily you would ask for the coordinator of volunteers. If the agency is small, there may be no coordinator and so you would ask for the director. He or she could recommend you to the appropriate person. If you have to leave a message, be sure to make a follow-up call yourself. Most service agencies are understaffed and very busy and it might be awhile before someone is able to get back to you.

When you do make contact with the appropriate person, explain that you are enrolled in a service program from your high school or parish. Ask if there are any volunteer opportunities. Arrange a personal interview with the coordinator and note the time and place of the volunteer orientation meeting. Treat this type of interview as you would an employment interview. Be prompt. Dress neatly. Also, be sure to bring along the commitment contract your school or parish requires. The agency will then know the stipulations of your commitment.

A key to any interview—be it on the phone or in person—is to be prepared. Have some idea of the kind of work the agency does and how you would be able to participate. What are your service work preferences? Though you may not get to do exactly what you would want, stating your preferences can help the supervisor match your talents to needed tasks. Clearly explain your time commitment. Outline all of the times you are and are not available. What do you hope to gain from your volunteer experience? Though this program may be required of you, be sure to express your willingness to being enriched in many new ways.

Also, it's always wise to have a list of prepared questions that *you* can ask at the interview. Here are a few:

1. Who is the staff member that will serve as my supervisor?

2. What will be my assigned schedule? How flexible are you in scheduling times?

3. Who would I call if I were unable to come on a given day?

4. Is there a dress code? What are some other procedures I need to know about?

5. Could I have a copy of the agency's mission statement, goals, or history to better familiarize myself before I begin?

At the conclusion of the interview, make sure you state your need to receive follow-up within a day or two. If this agency does not work out for whatever reason, you will need to find another. Remind the interviewer of your time frame.

Appreciate Your Uniqueness

While there are some poor reasons for choosing a service site ("I want to go where my friend goes" or "I want to work at an easy job"), most choices based on an honest reflection of your talents, gifts, and skills cannot be a wrong choice.

Everyone is unique. One person's gifts are not better than another's. All kinds of people are needed to make any kind of group or task function smoothly. As St. Paul wrote:

> There are different kinds of spiritual gifts but the same Spirit; there are different forms of service but the same Lord; there are different workings but the same God who produces all of them in everyone (1 Cor 12:4-7).

God created people with a variety of gifts so that they can best serve a variety of needs. Remember, there is some person or some project that is in need of the special gifts you have to offer. Take some time to reflect on where your personal gifts might best find expression. Talk with others, especially those who have done service before. Ask your friends to take account of your gifts and help you to choose an appropriate place. Also, remember that your service program director can help you if you have any doubts or hesitations about how to proceed.

activity 3-A

six steps for starting a conversation

No matter what your eventual service project or where your service site is, you will probably meet several new people. Part of your service may require taking the initiative to introduce yourself and begin a conversation. Take some time and review the following steps. Role play each step with a partner to get a feel for how they work.

1. Extend your hand, say "hello," and introduce yourself: for example, "I am . . ." or "My name is . . ."

2. Comment on something simple and obvious; the weather, an object in the room, or a well-known current event. Instead, you may just say something like, "This is my first time here" or "I have never been a part of a service program before."

3. Ask the person about himself or herself. This doesn't have to be too personal. You might say something like "How's your day been going so far?"

4. Continue the conversation by asking questions that give the other person the opportunity to expand on what is being said. Avoid questions with "yes" or "no" or one-word answers. Respond to the person's answers by smiling or nodding occasionally to show that you are really listening. Always try to maintain eye contact with the person.

5. When periods of silence do occur, move the conversation on to a new topic. The silent times will decrease once you get to know the person.

6. At the end of the conversation, say something like "It was nice to meet you" or "I'll look forward to talking with you again."

activity 3-B

choosing your ministry

Depending on the type of program you are in, you may be required to work at a designated service site or you may be choosing your own site. Even if you are assigned to a site, you will likely choose where you volunteer for ministry in the future. Complete the following questions to assist your search for the "right" ministry for you.

1. What are three types of volunteer activities that appeal to you?

   a.

   b.

   c.

2. List a reasonable schedule of times that you are free to do service during the course of a week.

3. What hesitancy, fear, or questions remain as you begin your service ministry?

4. Who is someone you know who has done volunteer service ministry? Share something of that person's experiences.

5. What individual, creative skills can you bring to a service ministry?

6. What do you hope to learn or become by doing service?

establishing objectives

OBJECTIVES:

- To understand the meaning and purpose of objectives
- To be familiar with techniques for developing immediate, mid-range, and long-term objectives
- To be patient with yourself and others at the service site

As you can see, each essay in this text has a list of objectives. You have probably encountered stated objectives in other areas of your life as well. Sometimes a coach of an athletic team will speak of objectives ("Our objective is to play strong defense.") or a family traveling on a vacation will have an objective ("We must travel 200 miles by the end of the day."). An objective is an *aim* or a *goal*. Setting predetermined objectives helps you to evaluate your progress and success. Establishing objectives is an important part of your participation in this service program too.

In establishing objectives, it's usually wise to take several views of what needs to be done. For example, you might have long-term, mid-range, and immediate objectives or goals. For a person assigned to visit a homebound parishioner, an immediate goal may be to simply make the visit as scheduled and to bring the person a favorite magazine or newspaper as a gift. Arranging a birthday celebration for the person in the upcoming month would be an example of a mid-range goal. A long-term goal might involve other people. In this case, it could include establishing a rotation in which other young people or adults take turns making visits to this person and other homebound parishioners.

Personalizing Your Goals

Answering the following questions can give you more insight into setting each type of objective for your service work.

What can my service accomplish? While there are limits to what one person can do, you need to know that your efforts are not futile. After all, the journey of a thousand miles begins with a single step! If everyone lamented "What can I possibly do about the problems and needs in the world?" and then did nothing, no good would ever be accomplished. Your efforts at Christian service—as small as they might seem to be—will allow some good to happen that would not occur if you were not in this program. Even if your service time is limited, the good that you do has real meaning and importance. In establishing immediate objectives, be precise and concrete. List in simple language two or three things that you hope to accomplish at each scheduled time. Run a mental checklist of these objectives as the session, visit, or meeting takes place. Look for ways to do the things you said that you would do.

How can I use my creativity? Immediate objectives usually translate to routine tasks. Mid-range objectives provide the chance for more creativity. At the outset, take some time to accustom yourself to the more basic tasks. Then, after you feel comfortable, brainstorm some ideas that would enhance your service opportunity. Write these ideas down on paper. Select one or two that are the most practical. Present these ideas to your supervisor. With him or her, choose one goal and set a target date for its completion. Make this plan your way of stamping your own personality on your service work. However, as you move to reach this goal, do not forget to maintain your immediate objectives and tasks.

How can I keep from being overwhelmed by the enormity of the problem? Long-term goals often seem like pipedreams; for example, "to eliminate the problem of homelessness in my city" or "to establish a hospice for AIDS patients at my parish." Long-term goals are often the expression of your innermost dreams and desires. These dreams are worthy and good. They can provide the spirit to your work. However, sometimes when young people enter service programs they become overwhelmed by the enormity of a huge problem they never realized existed before. One high school student who helped organize a Thanksgiving Day dinner for homeless people in her area was amazed by the number of families with young children who came. "I thought it would be old men with alcohol and drug abuse problems. I never imagined the problem reached so deep," she said. Problems you might have been aware of intellectually can become much too real once you actually begin to work with those in need.

Also, you may notice that people who work in difficult situations with little hope may often appear like they don't care as much as they should. They may even seem cynical about the major problem. But in all probability they have similar long-term objectives as you bring to your work. Because they chose to make a career out of service, they had to learn to distance themselves and not get too close to the people they serve. This is a behavior mechanism that can help a person to remain focused to the immediate and mid-range tasks while remaining mindful of the long-term objectives.

Don't be discouraged about setting long-term goals and objectives. But it might be wise not to want to contain them within the parameters of a defined amount of time. Your long-term objectives can be springboards for making the service you do in this program a life-long ministry.

What about me? An overriding objective of your service should be that your work will teach you something new about yourself. Involvement in service may help you to clarify whether or not you are more self-centered or other-centered. It may help you to see how you operate in new settings and how well you interact with people you are meeting for the first time. It might reveal personal qualities, talents, and skills that you never knew you had. Your commitment to this service program might help you to measure how well you are able to establish goals and then carry them out. Your service carries with it a certain sense of obligation—to the program, the service site supervisor, the people you serve—but also the creative freedom to make your mark in a new area. Be open to the experience and to what it can teach you!

writing objectives

Objectives should be written as a clear, concise statement of what you hope to accomplish by the end of a defined period of time. One technique is to write an objective statement beginning with the words "I will be able to . . ." Your objectives should be practical but at the same time challenging. Use the space below to practice writing immediate, mid-range, and long-term objectives for your service work. As you begin your project, update and add to these objectives as you proceed.

Immediate Objectives

1. I will be able to ______________________________

____

2. I will be able to ______________________________

____

Mid-range Objectives

1. I will be able to ______________________________

____

2. I will be able to ______________________________

____

Long-term Objectives

1. I will be able to ____

____

2. I will be able to ____

____

Updated Objectives

____

____

____

____

____

____

____

____

____

activity 4-B

performance checklist

Your immediate objectives are best evaluated soon after each visit to your service site. Ask yourself these questions at the end of each visit. Date and record notations in your notebook or journal.

1. How did I feel about coming to the site before I arrived (for example, apprehensive, excited, willing)? How did this initial feeling affect my performance?

2. What were my immediate objectives for this session? How do I rate my success in meeting these objectives?

3. How was I of most value? What was my least valuable time or activity?

4. How was I accountable to my service site supervisor? What do I need to discuss with my service site supervisor before I return?

5. How was I able to work at meeting my mid-range objectives? How was I able to work at my long-term objectives?

6. Where did I recognize God's presence? How well am I communicating to God in prayer about my experience?

7. What is something new I learned about myself?

8. How can this service be a part of my life after the program has been completed?

helping through listening

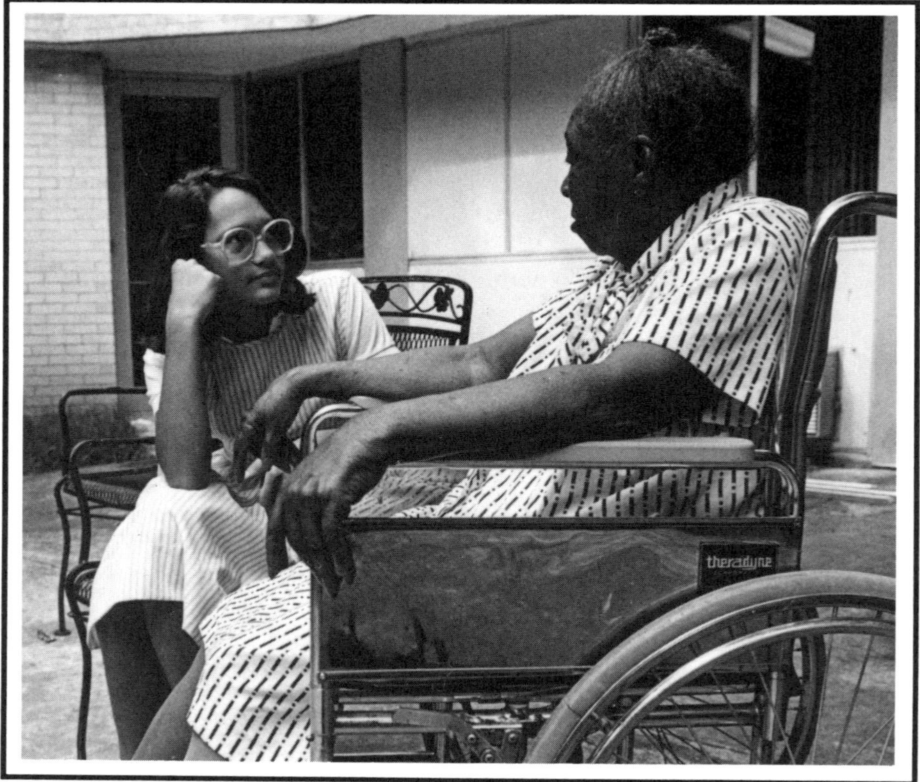

OBJECTIVES:

- To understand the meaning of compassion
- To be able to incorporate the ten listening skills into your own experience
- To grow in your skills as an empathetic listener

tuck in rush hour traffic on the busiest freeway in the city, Dana and Kerry were at least an hour away from school. To make matters worse, the radio in Kerry's old Volkswagen did not work.

Mrs. Freeman, the senior government teacher, had sent the two girls to the courthouse for the day to observe a criminal trial. Though Dana and Kerry had gone to school together for over eleven years, they really had never been friends. Neither hung out with the same group, and Dana knew that if her mom had let her borrow her car, well, she would have just as soon driven herself.

The day had gone smoothly, however. The girls had made small talk on the way down, had watched the trial in silence, and ate lunch with one of Mrs. Freeman's friends from the district attorney's office. Now, however, it seemed there was no way to avoid a deeper conversation.

It was Kerry who did all of the talking. Dana had asked about Kerry's brother, Ken, who had graduated the year before. Kerry began a story that would shock Dana; Ken had become addicted to drugs, was arrested in a robbery attempt, and now he was serving time in jail. Kerry told the story with emotion. When she shared how her brother's problems had affected her mother, she began to cry. Dana felt terrible because she didn't know what to say to lessen Kerry's pain. Mainly, Dana just sat in silence with a pained expression, nodding as a way of consolation.

That's why the next day Dana was surprised when Kerry greeted her at her locker early in the morning. "Thanks for all you did yesterday," Kerry said.

"But, I didn't do anything," Dana interrupted.

"Oh yes you did. You listened."

Compassion

Serving others is a real privilege. It gives you a good feeling, boosts your self-esteem, and makes you more aware of the struggles others have. Most often you cannot take away the pain or loneliness of someone else. But you can be *compassionate*. In Latin, compassion means "to suffer with." Service is often suffering with others, being with them in their pain. Think about times that you have had your own problems. How have your friends been of help?

One of the best ways for a person to be compassionate is to be a good listener. Being a good listener is not as simple as it seems. It is actually a self-discipline and skill that must be cultivated and practiced. As you continue in this service program, try to make listening one of the skills that you master. You will likely be asked to listen to the people you serve. You will need to listen to the people you work for. And, you are asked to listen to the successes and failures of others in your group as they work through their own projects. Like Kerry, most people need someone to air out their life stories with from time to time. Here are ten steps that can help you to improve your listening skills:

1. Make eye contact with the person throughout the conversation.

2. Nod your head occasionally or say things like "I see" or "I understand" to show that you are following the flow of the conversation.

3. Don't interrupt with unnecessary information that detracts from what the speaker is saying.

4. Listen for the deeper feelings beneath the words that are being spoken.

5. Summarize what the person has said and ask for clarification of ideas and feelings that have been expressed. For example, if an elderly person tells you how nobody comes to visit, you might try to summarize by saying, "You must be lonely here. I hope that changes for you."

6. Don't ask questions that are too personal. Rather, ask questions that invite more speaking like "Could you tell me more about that?" or "What did you do about that situation?"

7. Don't judge or act shocked or horrified by certain information. When people are criticized, they tend to not want to continue.

8. Don't lecture or give little pep talks. Also, avoid using clichés like "tomorrow's another day" or "there are more fish in the sea." As you probably know from your own experience, these clichés are rarely helpful.

9. Don't give advice or tell people what they should do to solve their problems. If people don't choose their own solutions, they never really "own" them. It's fine to make suggestions beginning with phrases like "Have you ever thought of . . ." or "Have you tried . . .", but clearly recognize that being a good listener does not mean being a problem-solver.

10. Keep what is told to you confidential. The exception to this rule is when you are given information that leads you to believe the person is a threat to himself or herself or another (for example, if a person is suicidal or plotting to hurt someone else). Clearly, in these instances you should report what you have heard to your service program director or service site supervisor.

Good listening can be summed up in one word: *empathy*. Empathy means putting yourself in someone else's place and imagining how it must feel to be in their situation. The other person's feelings trigger similar feelings in you. For example, if an elderly person is crying because she is lonely, you may realize that you have many fears about being lonely too. If a teenager detained in a juvenile rehabilitation center shares the hurt that he has caused his parents, you may take a look at your own relationship with your mother or father. Being empathetic means that a good listener must not only be in touch with the other person's feelings, but must also listen to his or her own feelings that their story is stirring up. As these feelings arise, it will be important for you to write about them in your journal or share them as part of a group discussion.

open questions

Given the information provided, invent an *open question* that invites the speaker to expand on what was said and answer with more than a "yes" or "no" response.

1. My mother's new boyfriend is kind of strange. I mean I like him well enough, but he's always bossing me around.

Open question:

____

____

____

2. My best friend and I haven't spoken for the last month. I don't care if I ever see her again.

Open question:

____

____

____

3. This place is so lonely. Nobody ever talks to me and my family only visits once a month.

Open question:

____

____

____

4. This country is all messed up. You would think that a veteran of the war could find a decent job.

Open question:

____

____

____

5. It's taken a long time to get used to being in a wheelchair. I still have some days when I feel very frustrated.

Open question:

____

____

____

activity 5-B

what else is being said?

Being a good listener often means "reading between the lines" of what is being said. Read the statements below. Write a summary of the feelings behind what is being said.

1. This school is no good. The people here are all stuck up. I don't want to be their friend anyway.

____

____

2. I'm happy my best friend and her boyfriend get along so well. I can always find someone to go skiing with.

____

____

3. Burger World used to be a great place to hang out. I have really seen it go down in the past few years. Since I stopped working there, I have not gone to Burger World like I once did.

____

____

4. I'm glad I didn't get accepted into that college. I don't think I would want to live away from home.

____

____

5. She's really smart. She rarely studies and always gets the best grades. Meanwhile, all I ever seem to do is study yet I never get higher than average marks.

____

____

keeping a journal

OBJECTIVES:

- To examine some of the benefits of keeping a journal
- To see journal writing as a form of prayer
- To consider situations in which you might share a journal entry with another
- To learn a format for keeping a journal entry

ne way that people can clarify problems and look for the right solutions is by talking with a good listener. Another is to record their daily happenings in a *journal*. The word journal really means "book of days." Writing in a journal fulfills much of the same need as talking with a good listener in that it helps you release the experience so that you can understand it more as an observer would, from the outside looking in.

Your service program director will probably require you to keep a journal. If not, it would be a good idea for you to begin keeping journal entries on your own. Purchase a separate notebook to use for your Christian service experiences. Then, within a day after you return from your service project site, record some of the things that happened and how you felt about the experience. Date your entry. By the end of the program, you will be able to make note of the different kinds of experiences and feelings you had.

Another benefit of writing in a journal is that it allows you to pray through your writing. Entire entries can be addressed in prayer to Jesus. You can ask Jesus questions. You can write directly to Jesus about the things that are happening. You can bring to Jesus the needs of those you serve. You can thank Jesus for the ways you have been able to find his face in those who are poor, joyful, needy, and happy. As the poet Gerard Manley Hopkins wrote: "Christ plays in ten thousand places. Lovely in limbs and lovely in eyes not his." How does this quotation relate to your own service work?

You can take your reflection on the life of Jesus a step further. Use the work you do to learn more about Jesus' own life and his model of service while on earth. Choose a section of a gospel that tells something about Jesus and what he did. Imagine yourself as Jesus or one of the other characters in the scene. For example, you might take the role of Jesus as he heals a person who is sick or the role of a sinner who has received Jesus' forgiveness. In your journal, record your feelings. Finally, ask yourself: "What does this gospel story have to do with my service project? How have I witnessed Jesus in this role? Who are the people I work with that need the healing touch that Jesus offers?"

In addition to recording your experiences at your service site you can also use a journal to keep a collection of meaningful advice someone has given you, quotations that you read, a lesson that you learned, or even one line of a song lyric that stayed with you throughout a particular day. Record these sayings. Elaborate in writing why they are meaningful to you. God speaks to you in many ways. Sometimes it is a matter of simply pausing to note a message from God that has been placed right before your eyes.

Journal Format

If keeping a journal is a required part of your service program, it will likely be read by the service program director or shared in class or with a small group. You might want to ask the service program director to clarify who will read each entry. You can then write accordingly, even wishing to save some very personal entries for another place, or marking them so that your director knows that you do not wish them shared with anyone else.

Sharing journal entries can be a good source of encouragement, learning, and healing. The advantage of having your service program director review your journal is that he or she can assess your growth during the experience and also help you to clarify some of your important questions and issues. If your journal is shared with a partner, small group, or the entire class, you will have the advantage of hearing how your experiences often parallel with those of others. You will be able to share how your experiences differ. The main benefit of sharing your reflections with others is that it makes this a more shared journey than a private one. You might realize more clearly that what you are doing is a community effort in the name of Christ and his disciples.

There are many formats for keeping journal entries. You may vary your entries from time to time, or keep the same format. It is a good idea to date each entry so that you can more closely track your development. Here is one standard format you may wish to use:

Title (optional)

Date: ______________________________

Service site: ____

Two important things I did today:

Something meaningful that someone said to me:

One way that I experienced God's presence was:

A prayerful thought of the day:

Rather than use a specific format, you may prefer to simply write in your journal in paragraph form, summarizing your experiences and reflecting on what occurred. Remember, your journal should fulfill many of the same needs that a good listener does. And, just as there are many different ways to be a good listener, there are many different kinds of good journals. Proceed!

activity 6-A

gospel reflections

Listed below are several gospel passages having to do with the theme of service. Choose one or more to use as a starting point for a journal entry. After reading the passage, write your answers to the following questions or your own personal reflection. Record your entry in your journal.

Matthew 5:3-12 (The Beatitudes)

Matthew 6:1-4 (Teaching about Almsgiving)

Matthew 8:5-13 (Healing of the Centurion's Servant)

Mark 2:1-12 (Healing of the Paralytic)

Mark 6:34-44 (Feeding of the Five Thousand)

Luke 10:29-42 (Parable of the Good Samaritan)

Luke 15:11-32 (Parable of the Lost Son)

John 2:1-12 (Wedding at Cana)

John 11:1-44 (Raising of Lazarus)

John 13:1-20 (Washing of the Disciples' Feet)

Questions:

1. How do you identify with Jesus or one of the other characters in the passage?

2. What does this gospel story have to do with your service project?

3. How have you witnessed Jesus in this role?

4. Who are the people you work with that need the healing touch that Jesus offers?

activity 6-B

listening and recording

Part of the skill of keeping a journal is being able to take the time to review your day, oftentimes from the perspective of seeing the extraordinary in the ordinary, of God in the faces of people and events. Practice this skill by looking back at the past twenty-four hours in your life. Write your reflections to the following:

What was the most meaningful advice someone told you?

How did you witness or experience suffering? What did the suffering teach you about God?

How did you witness or experience joy? What did the joy teach you about God?

What is something someone told you, something you read, something you saw on television, or something you heard in a song that communicated a positive message to you?

How did you help another? How did someone help you?

From what you learned today, what is a resolution you can make for tomorrow?

working with a support group

OBJECTIVES:

- To appreciate the need for belonging to a peer support group when undertaking Christian service ministry
- To examine several issues that might be explored in a peer support group format
- To understand the concept of "co-dependency" as related to doing service

A peer support group is primarily the place to share the positive experiences you've had in Christian service with people your own age. In this program, the peer support group may be another name for your religion class, your confirmation group, or your youth ministry group. Or, it may be a smaller group of your peers who are also a part of one of those larger groups. In any case, sometimes when you do something that is new, it's hard to know if what you are feeling is common to others or unique to yourself. Meetings with a peer support group can help to differentiate between both kinds of feelings.

There is no doubt that not all of your work at a Christian service site has gone smoothly. You have probably had some negative experiences too. But, generally, if you are participating in a program that has as its main objective the help and service of others, you might feel satisfied at a job well done or that you are at least making some positive difference in the world. The smile or grateful look in someone's eyes when you arrive or depart from your service site might mean quite a bit to you. You may have received a compliment from someone on a job well done. Maybe you even received a surprise gift on one of your visits. Or, you discovered a new talent you never knew you had, or a new sensitivity or interest for a particular issue or way of life. These are the types of things that need to be shared with a support group. You should tell of these uplifting moments. You need to hear about the successes of others. This type of sharing and support can make your Christian service participation much more worthwhile.

Certainly, a support group can also help you to relieve the stress of your work (or any stress in your life). When you have a really difficult experience at your service site, sharing what happened with your support group can help. Something that happened to you at your service site may have awakened some personal anxieties. For example, visits to a nursing home may recall feelings about a grandparent who has recently died. Or, serving meals to the homeless and desolate may lead a person to wonder where his or her own parent's drinking or drug problem will lead. Sharing personal problems of this kind with your support group can help you to reduce your stress and bear your pressures more easily. If you feel uncomfortable about sharing with a group, another option is to share these types of anxieties with your program service director. The bottom line is that you should not keep these problems to yourself.

Talking about personal problems or general stress on the job can also be beneficial because it can teach you to be more compassionate of others. Remember that the meaning of ministry is to be compassionate, or suffer with people in their pain. In your service ministry, you may sometimes say the wrong thing, or say nothing because you just don't have any clue about what words might help. You may feel like an outsider, like nothing you can do there has any real effect on anyone. Maybe the problem area you have chosen just seems too big or hopeless. No matter what you do, no positive change seems to result. These so-called "failures" are certainly material to talk over at a peer support group meeting. Ask others in the group if they are having the same kinds of experiences you are. You may also wish to talk over struggles like:

- a personality conflict with someone at your service site;
- the pressure of arranging a service schedule around your job, sports, family duties, or other extracurricular activities;
- the feeling that you lack the skills to be an effective minister;
- the notion that you aren't making a difference (for example, the elderly lady you visit with each week never even remembers who you are);
- the overwhelming social problem that underlies the work you are doing;
- not being able to meet everyone's demands (for example, a group of little children you care for never want you to leave);
- confusion over a vocational calling (for example, you may like the thought of being a social worker, but you also want to earn a good salary);
- being "burned out"; you have no energy left and no more to offer;
- feelings of sadness, depression, and helplessness that doing service has generated in you.

Co-Dependency

A support group can help you avoid being co-dependent in your ministry. Co-dependency is a term borrowed from the field of addictions. It means that even though you might not personally have an addiction, your behavior could contribute to the addiction of another. The classic example is of one spouse who covers up for the husband or wife's alcohol or drug addiction. This person's behavior contributes to the other's addiction. Why wouldn't this person confront the problem? Addiction theory would say that it is because the spouse of the addict desperately *needs to be needed,* to have someone to care for and worry about. The root of this neediness is low self-esteem.

How does this relate to service? A person should not commit to service only as a means to have his or her needs fulfilled. Recall that people are made worthwhile for who they are, not what they do. People who "need to be needed" may require this affirmation as a way to feel good about themselves. They may only feel worthwhile when someone else tells them that they have done *something* good, not that they themselves *are* good.

Community of Faith

This task that you have undertaken should not be one that is accomplished alone. Jesus' ministry of service was not done alone. Jesus was very deliberate about choosing a group of followers to accompany him on his mission. The church has not only continued Jesus' outreach to others, but has done so in communion with one another. The church's ministry of service is not a solitary one. One way to imagine the function of the peer support group for your service ministry is to look at how the sacraments—especially the eucharist—function for the community of believers. The eucharist is a deep source of strength and support for Christians living the life of Christ. They gather to greet one another, pray together, and receive nourishment from Jesus in the word of God and in his body and blood. Your support group can function in a similar way.

activity 7-A

keeping in touch

A benefit of a peer support group is that it provides a means for sharing experiences. Also, peer support group members can many times network with one another to build on work already being done or to develop structures for new programs. Use the space below to record the first and last names of peer support group members you work closely with, their phone numbers, and a word to remind you of their special area of interest.

Name	Phone Number	Area of Interest

activity 7-B

working together

The success of Jesus' ministry depended on the help he received from others. Luke's gospel tells how Jesus sent his disciples in pairs to preach the good news in his name. Read the following passage. Then write what you think each of the highlighted phrases mean in relation to the gospel text and your own service ministry.

> The Lord appointed seventy-two others whom he sent ahead of him in pairs to every town and place he intended to visit. He said to them, "The harvest is abundant but the laborers are few; so ask the master of the harvest to send out laborers for his harvest. Go on your way; behold I am sending you like lambs among wolves. Carry no money bag, no sack, no sandals; and greet no one along the way. Into whatever house you enter, first say, 'Peace to this household.' If a peaceful person lives there, your peace will rest on him; but if not, it will return to you. Stay in the same house and eat and drink what is offered to you, for the laborer deserves his payment. Do not move about from one house to another. Whatever town you enter and they welcome you, eat what is set before you, cure the sick in it and say to them, 'The kingdom of God is at hand for you.'"
>
> —Luke 10:1-9

. . . he sent ahead of him in pairs.

. . . The harvest is abundant but the laborers are few.

. . . I am sending you like lambs among wolves.

. . . Do not move around from one house to another.

. . . The kingdom of God is at hand for you.

prayer: the source of service

OBJECTIVES:

- To understand the similarities and differences between Christian service ministry and other humanitarian efforts
- To become familiar with the terms "grace" and "reign of God"
- To see the necessity of prayer in a life of committed service
- To examine various kinds of prayers and the effect of prayer in one service situation

s you may have noticed, there are lots of good people doing good things. At your very service site you have probably met people who are dedicated to a life of serving a worthy cause and serving other people. Also, people generally have good motives for any project or life work they undertake. Given these facts, you may wonder about the necessity of God and religion in conjunction with doing service.

Certainly, there is nothing different on the surface between Christian service ministry and secular social work. Many people choose service careers like social work, medicine, or teaching for *humanitarian* reasons, that is, "the service of humanity." Your service program is designed to meet people's needs. The difference between Christian service and other humanitarian efforts is that a Christian's motivation also hinges on building up the reign of God. This means that Christian service has a transcendent dimension; what you do in this world not only effects the here and now, but also serves in building God's reign in the next world as well. Authentic Christian service is motivated by a person's faith and by God's *grace.*

Grace is another word to describe "God's life." Through grace, you are given a new perspective of people and events as if you are looking at them through the eyes of God. This new perspective can best be summed up in one word: *love.* In love, Christians are called in a special way to do many things that would seem unnatural without the right motivation. After you die, Jesus said that the way you will be judged is in how well you have loved:

> "For I was hungry and you gave me food, I was thirsty and you gave me drink, a stranger and you welcomed me, naked and you clothed me, in prison and you visited me" (Mt 25:35-36).

In addition, Christian love is measured in how well you loved the "least" members of society. Jesus added, "Whatever you did for one of these least ones, you did for me" (Mt 25:40).

How can you go about acquiring the grace needed to love and serve others? Certainly, your participation in a Christian community is an important source of grace. Jesus said:

> "For where two or three are gathered in my name, there am I in the midst of them" (Mt 18:20).

For example, Jesus is present at each meeting of your class, youth group, or peer support group. Also, celebrating the eucharist and the other sacraments is an energizing source of grace that can help you to be faithful to a life committed to love.

Benefits of Prayer

The most common source of grace is prayer, either personal or communal prayer. A traditional church expression teaches of "offering up" one's thoughts, words, and actions to God. This means that everything a person does is done in God's name. Your personal prayer can take many forms, including:

Petitionary. These are often known as "prayers of asking." You ask God to be with you and fulfill your needs.

Intercessory. In prayers of intercession, you pray for others. When people ask you to pray for them and their needs and you oblige, you are praying an intercessory prayer.

Thanksgiving. You offer thanks to God for the graces and gifts of your life.

Praise. You laud God's glory and greatness. Often, you are able to recognize God's splendor in the beauty of creation, especially through the lives of other people. You praise God when you shout out to the glory of all the wonderful things that God has done.

Prayer, of course, can take place at any time; prayer as part of your participation in this service program can likewise take place at a variety of times *and* places. Pray any form of prayer whenever and wherever it comes natural to you: in the morning, in the evening, in your car, or when you are alone. Tell God about your disappointments, your fears, your successes, and about the wonderful people you meet. If you are working directly with people, take them also by name to God in prayer. You will be amazed at the difference between doing service *with* prayer than *without* it. You will also notice a new energy that you are given when you take your daily needs, gratefulness, and praise to God.

Testimony to the benefits of prayer with service is offered in this story of Terry and Bill. Terry was a high school senior assigned to weekly visits of Bill at a rehabilitation hospital. Bill had been in a bad car accident and had multiple injuries, including some brain damage. His prognosis for ever being able to leave the hospital was poor.

Terry, meanwhile, would come to visit Bill each week. Invariably, Bill would ask Terry her name. Then, the two would play checkers in virtual silence. This routine went on for almost two months.

Finally, Terry's frustration was revealed at her peer support group meeting. "I come to visit him every week and he doesn't even remember my name," Terry told her friends. At the end of the session the group prayed for Terry's needs and for Bill. They encouraged Terry to continue to pray before she went back to the hospital.

Nothing changed right away, but three weeks later Terry walked into Bill's room and found him playing checkers with another patient. For a minute the two men didn't even look up from their game. Terry became even more angry. Then, Bill sat up straight and said to the other patient matter-of-factly, "This is my friend Terry. She comes and plays checkers with me every week." Terry's spirit was moved with joy and the struggles of the first visits, for that one moment, were all worth it. Terry remembered the prayer of her support group and her personal prayer. From that time on, prayer became a vital part of her time spent in service with Bill.

While it is certainly possible to accomplish good works without prayer, the grace of God that results from prayer is a way to remove all self-centeredness from the mission to serve. God's grace can provide you with the strength to persevere in your service and the insight to appreciate the good that you do.

activity 8-A

prayer inspirations

The following are inspirational reflections related to the theme of service. Read one at a time. Use it as a source of grace or as a starting point for a prayer-filled entry in your journal.

1. "The opposite of love is not hatred; it is indifference."

—Daniel Berrigan, S.J.

St. John Of The Cross

2. "In the evening of this life you will be judged according to your love."

—St. John of the Cross

3. "The worst of partialities is to withhold oneself; the worst of ignorance is not to act; the worst lie is to steal away."

—Peguy

4. "When I give food to the poor, they call me a saint. When I ask why the poor have no food they call me a communist."

—Dom Helder Camara

5. "That I feed the hungry, that I forgive an insult, that I love my enemy in the name of Christ, all these are undoubtedly great virtues. What I do unto the least of my brethren, that I do unto Christ. But what if I should discover that the least among them all, the poorest of beggars . . . the very enemy himself, that these are within me, and that I myself stand in the need of the alms of my own kindness—that I myself am the enemy who must be loved—what then?"

—C.J. Jung

6. "If I am not for myself who will be? If I am only for myself, what will I become?"

—Hillel

St. Thérèse of Lisieux

7. "Remember that nothing is small in the eyes of God. Do all that you do with love."

—St. Thérèse of Lisieux

8. Small service is true service while it lasts:
Of humblest friends, bright Creature!
scorn not one;
The Daisy, by the shadow it casts,
Protects the lingering dew drop
from the Sun.

—Wordsworth

9. "Jesus is a path, if any be misled; he is robe of any naked be; if any chance to hunger, he is bread."

—Giles Fletcher, Jr.

10. "We have all known the long loneliness and we have learned that the only solution is love and that love comes with community."

—Dorothy Day

Dorothy Day

activity 8-B

sources of meditation

Look up each of these scripture passages in the Bible. Write a one sentence summary of each passage. Tell a specific way that it relates to your own service.

1. **Acts 4:32-35**

2. **Micah 6:8**

3. **Matthew 6:1-4**

4. **Matthew 25:31-46**

5. **John 15:13**

6. **1 Corinthians 12:5-6**

7. **2 Corinthians 9:6-9**

8. **James 2:14-17**

the path to advocacy: the next step

OBJECTIVES:

- To help you examine the lessons learned from your direct service
- To recall that serving others is a part of your baptismal vocation
- To understand the distinction between charity and advocacy
- To think about how you are called to continue your service efforts

At baptism, you or your parents were given a lighted candle from the Easter candle and told to "walk always as children of the light." Your time in a service *program* is ending, but your vocation to serve others extends for a lifetime. What did being in a program teach you about service? Did it:

- help you to realize how many opportunities there are for service in your parish, neighborhood, and community?
- provide a framework for guidance and support and the opportunity to pray and reflect on your service?
- introduce you to new people you might never of had a chance to meet?
- teach you skills that you will be able to use in future endeavors?
- encourage you to integrate the service of others into all areas of your life?

What are some other things you learned from participating in the service program? What does your baptismal call to walk as a child of the light have to do with serving others? The focus of this essay is to examine ways that you can move from program-oriented service to service that is a natural part of your life.

Charity and Advocacy

Your service in this program has probably been in the area of *charity*. Charity means to "love people in God's name." Charity is expressed in "direct service," doing things like visiting the elderly, collecting clothes for the poor, or tutoring a child who needs help with schoolwork. Charity is a way to help others cope with their present crisis or life situation.

You probably know something of the story of Mother Teresa. She began a religious community to help the destitute and dying on the streets of India. Her works of charity led to deeper questions: "Why is there so much poverty in India? Why do the poor have no access to medical treatment? What's wrong with political structures that allow situations like this to exist?" It is perfectly logical and normal for your direct service experience to lead you to questions of fairness and justice because many times the surface problems of society belie underlying social ills.

Working to remove the deeper problem is called *advocacy*. An advocate is someone "who speaks or writes for the cause of another." For example, if you have been doing direct service at a home for the elderly, you may have been visiting the residents, bringing them reading materials, taking them for walks. On your visits you may have noticed that the room temperature at the facility where they stay is always much too cool. Direct service would move you to bring a room heater for the one or two people you specifically visit. As an advocate, however, you would seek a cure for the larger problem. You would speak with the site supervisor about the problem. He or she might refer you to the owner of the facility. You could then write or call the owner to explain the problem.

Charity doesn't always lead to advocacy, but it often does. If your heart is moving you toward advocacy because of your direct service work you should discuss your thoughts with your service program director and your peer support group. Advocacy is usually a difficult task to undertake alone. Most advocates choose to affiliate with a group of people with common goals. You may have advocate groups in your school or parish; Students Against Drunk Driving (S.A.D.D.), Amnesty International, and the St. Vincent de Paul Society are examples.

Some people are called more to charity than advocacy, and vice versa. Some people are called to both. Mother Teresa has a clear vocation to charity, to the direct service of the pressing needs of individuals. Cesar Chávez, the late founder of the United Farm Workers Union, chose the path of advocacy to affect the change of the deplorable conditions faced by migrant workers. Dorothy Day was an example of a person who did direct service to the poor and was also their advocate. She not only established shelters for homeless people, but she published a newspaper called the *Catholic Worker* which was to be an agent of social change.

Where do you feel your primary calling lies? Are you a person who would more readily participate in an AIDS walk-a-thon to raise money for the cure of the disease than care for a dying AIDS patient? If so, your calling may be to advocacy. Or, are you a person who would prefer counseling pregnant teenage girls than writing a letter to your representative protesting lenient abortion laws? If so, you may be called more to charity. Or, you may be like Dorothy Day and feel the call to both styles of Christian service. Hopefully, your time in this service program has given you new clues to your talents and new insights into how you will use your gifts to meet the needs of others. Both charity and advocacy are essential in terms of Christian service. Each helps to fulfill your baptismal vocation to "keep God's commandments as Christ taught us, by loving God and our neighbor."

activity 9-A

charity or advocacy?

Use the chart to list typical qualities of people attracted to direct service through charity and qualities of people attracted to service through advocacy. After developing these stereotypical profiles, ask yourself how you fit in to both categories. Are you more likely to prefer a service role of charity or advocacy? Use the writing lines to explain. Share your reasoning with a partner or your peer support group.

Qualities	Charity	Advocacy
Personality	1. 2. 3.	1. 2. 3.
Skills	1. 2. 3.	1. 2. 3.
Interests	1. 2. 3.	1. 2. 3.

Charity or Advocacy? My Preference

activity 9-B

path to advocacy spectrum

Moving from direct service to advocacy is possible with most areas of direct service. Use this chart to show a workable flow from service to advocacy.

Choose three direct service areas (for example, from those areas chosen by members of your peer support group). Write these in the column labeled "form of direct service." Then, take some time to fill out the rest of the chart for each service area. Share your ideas with the appropriate members of your group.

Form of Direct Service:	Skills or Qualities Needed:	The Underlying Social Problem:	Skills or Qualities Needed for Advocacy:	Name of an established Advocacy Group:

CHARITY ——————————→ ADVOCACY

CHARITY ——————————→ ADVOCACY

CHARITY ——————————→ ADVOCACY

termination and evaluation

OBJECTIVES:

- To learn appropriate ways to end your commitment to the service program and service site
- To understand how you will be evaluated by others
- To be able to offer an honest self-evaluation of your participation in the service program

Whereas your responsibility to service is part of a lifetime *process*, participation in a *program* of this kind has a definite beginning and an end. You have now reached the conclusion. Let your service site supervisor and co-workers know the date of your last visit at least one week ahead of time. Also, let any people you have ministered to know that soon you will not be visiting them anymore. You may have built some relationships at your service site that will make this separation difficult for you. Here are some general suggestions:

1. *Don't make unrealistic promises.* It's commendable to want to continue visiting someone or doing volunteer work after your service program has officially ended, but don't make unrealistic promises that you won't be able to keep. If you are going to a new school or if your work or sport schedules will not allow it, don't promise something that you will not realistically be able to follow through on. It's better to undergo the initial pain of a difficult separation than to eventually not be able to keep a promise. Also, be sure to check with your service site supervisor before you make plans to continue your service at your present location.

2. *Say the appropriate farewells.* Don't just slip away never to reappear. Make arrangements to say good-bye to the people you worked with and for. Also, you should make a special effort to thank your service site supervisor. Do this in person and with a written thank-you note.

3. *Discuss the termination experience with your peer support group.* Offer support to one another, especially concerning severed relationships. If you are considering being part of an advocacy effort and no group is currently established in your area of interest, inquire among your peer support group members of their willingness to help you organize and participate in a new group.

4. *Don't feel guilty if you feel happy or relieved that the program is over.* Perhaps the service site you chose or were assigned was not tailored to your creativity, your interests, or your energy level. Maybe the most important lesson you learned was that there are some types of service ministry that are not meant for you. If this has been your experience, be honest with your feelings and express them with your peer support group.

Evaluation

A final part of the service program is a series of evaluations. You may have already been evaluated at certain stages by your service program director or your service site supervisor. As the final evaluations of your performance commence, you will be evaluated based on some or all of the following:

1. Your faithfulness to your time commitment;
2. Your energy level of involvement at the service site;
3. Your willingness to learn about others and to experience new things;

4. Your ability to work together (at the service site and with your peer support group);

5. Your personal growth.

In addition, your service program director may be evaluating your journal, any time spent with you in group sessions or individual conferences, and feedback he or she received personally from the service site supervisor.

Your own self-evaluation of your performance is critical. Though you may have been a part of a peer support group or a class and worked as a member of a volunteer staff, you may have found your service work to be a very personal, private experience. After all, you may have chosen your area of service yourself. You may have been the only one from your group at your service site. You may have done much of your work with people on a one-to-one basis.

On the next pages, you will be asked to *describe* and *analyze* the work you did. You will also be asked to reflect on the *spiritual dimension* of the program and how your own faith life was affected by the work you did. Your responses to these questions should be shared with your peer support group. Then, you will be asked to fill out a self-evaluation. Your service program director may ask you to share all or part of this with him or her as a way to help in determining your overall evaluation. As you prepare for your own self-evaluation, be thinking about these questions:

1. How was I faithful to my commitment?

2. How much effort did I put into my service?

3. What is something about others I learned doing service?

4. What is something about myself I learned doing service?

5. How did my service affect my relationship with God?

Finally, you will be asked to offer an evaluation for your service program site and the service program itself. Take time to answer these questions carefully. Some of the suggestions and other feedback you offer can be used as a benefit for not only the service site, but for future students from your school or parish who may choose to volunteer there in the future.

activity 10-A

christian service reflections

Part 1: Description

1. Briefly summarize your project (for example, the name of the agency, frequency of your service, what your duties were):

2. Write about one or two of the most memorable people you worked with or worked for.

Part 2: Analysis

1. Evaluate any change in your attitude about service from the beginning of the program to now.

2. Evaluate your effectiveness objectively. Rate your attitude, your rapport with people, your sense of responsibility, and your usefulness to the agency or a particular person you served.

3. List one personal strength and one personal weakness you discovered about yourself while participating in this program.

4. What was the most significant experience you had while volunteering? Explain why it was significant to you.

5. What advice can you offer another volunteer who might choose this area of service? this service site? Be specific.

Part 3: Spiritual Dimension

1. What did you learn about Jesus' model of service and gospel values by participating in this program?

2. Tell one way you experienced God's presence through your work or the people you served.

activity 10-B

student self-evaluation

Name: ____________________

School/Parish: ____________________

Service Program Director: ____________________

Project Site/Description: ____________________

Grade yourself on each item using the following scale:

1 — maximum effort
2 — above average effort
3 — adequate effort
4 — below average effort
5 — minimal effort

1. I analyzed my talents and gifts before choosing a service project.

1 2 3 4 5

2. I consulted with others—including my service program director—about my choice of a service project and site.

1 2 3 4 5

3. I made prayer a part of my service work.

1 2 3 4 5

4. I took time to prepare for my interview and/or orientation at the service site.

1 2 3 4 5

5. I cooperated with the service site supervisor.

1 2 3 4 5

6. I was careful about coming to the service site with a positive attitude.

1 2 3 4 5

7. I focused on the person or job at hand rather than the amount of time I had spent at the service site or working on the project.

1 2 3 4 5

8. I have applied what I have learned in the service program to other relationships and areas of my life.

1 2 3 4 5

9. I was conscientious about keeping a journal as a record of my reflections on service.

1 2 3 4 5

10. I shared my honest feelings with my peer support group.

1 2 3 4 5

11. I worked at being a more effective listener, both with my peer support group and with the people I worked with.

1 2 3 4 5

12. I have taken the evaluation process seriously.

1 2 3 4 5

Add your scores. Divide the total score by the number of items that were applicable to your experience. Round the average to the nearest whole number. On the lines below, explain why or why not this grade honestly reflects the amount of effort you put into the program.

part 2

appendix

journal entry 1

before

Think about your motivation to serve. Write about some of the reasons you have agreed to be in this program.

____

____

____

____

____

____

____

List five things you are looking forward to and five things you are dreading about being a service participant.

1. ____________________	1. ____________________
2. ____________________	2. ____________________
3. ____________________	3. ____________________
4. ____________________	4. ____________________
5. ____________________	5. ____________________

Read the "servant of the Lord" song from Isaiah 49:1-7. Reflect on how you are special in the eyes of God. What qualities of servant leadership do you have?

journal entry 2

before

Imagine this scene: as you make preparations for your service, you decide to make a visit to a local home for the elderly. A wise old woman—eighty-six-year-old Maggie—watches from her window as you come up the walk. She sees much more than your outward appearance. She can tell lots about your feelings, dreams, goals, and desires. Write what Maggie sees. Describe the *real* you.

These sketches show people of three different age groups, each with different needs. Which age group or need would you feel most comfortable serving? Explain what you would do for the person below that you chose to serve.

journal entry 3

during

A phone introduction might be your ticket in to or out of a service opportunity. Write a script that introduces yourself, tells about your service program and what you need of a service site, and describes how your talents might serve the particular agency. Practice and remember what you wrote. Use this introduction when you arrange an orientation or service site interview by phone.

Sensory Impressions

You've made your first trip to your service site. Record your first impressions of:

Sight

____

____

____

____

Sound

____

____

____

____

Smells

____

____

____

____

Touch

____

____

____

____

Taste(?)(!)

____

____

____

____

journal entry 4

during

The journey of a thousand miles began with a single step. Write about your "first step"—the details of your first visit to your service site. (Share both the good things that happened and the not so good.)

Write one amazing fact about the agency, service site supervisor, or person you serve that you would have never known if you hadn't taken this assignment:

NERVOUS Excited helpful
TIRED SHOCKED AMAZED
CONFUSED Loved USELESS
Happy
comfortable HORRIFIED GREAT
lost DISCOMBOBULATED

Use one of these adjectives or one of your own as a title for a reflection on your initial experiences of service. Write your reflection here:

journal entry 5

during

Read the scripture passage. Write your responses to the questions that follow.

> Then the Lord said to Elijah, "Go outside and stand on the mountain before the Lord; the Lord will be passing by." A strong and heavy wind was rending the mountains and crushing rocks before the Lord—but the Lord was not in the wind. After the wind there was an earthquake—but the Lord was not in the earthquake. After the earthquake there was fire—but the Lord was not in the fire. After the fire there was a tiny whispering sound. When he heard this, Elijah hid his face in his cloak and went and stood before the entrance of the cave.
>
> —1 Kings 19:11-12

How has God been revealed to you?

____

____

How have you been surprised by God's appearance?

____

____

What is God trying to say to you?

____

____

Write about a time you were an effective listener.

____

____

Write a prayer to help you in your ministry. Use these letters to begin the first word of each line.

S ____

E ____

R ____

V ____

E ____

journal entry 6

during

Write a set of lyrics or a refrain from a song that resonates with your experience in service ministry. If you wish, also tell why these words have special meaning to you.

Share a piece of advice you were given about your service work.
How did you feel about receiving this advice?
According to this advice, what are you called to do?
How will you do it?

Problem Prayer

Write a prayer about, for, to, because of, or how to avoid a problem you have encountered in your service ministry.

journal entry 7

during

Write the names of the people in your peer support group. Next to each person's name, write one word that can help you recall one new thing you have learned about yourself, others, or God from them and their stories.

Write about one time you experienced the "need to be needed."

The centurion said:

> "Lord, I am not worthy to have you enter under my roof;
> only say the word and my servant will be healed."

Read the complete text of this story from Matthew 8:5-13. What does this story tell you about Jesus' service ministry?

journal entry 8

during

Grace

Write a story, poem, prayer, reflection, or share some simple examples of how God's grace has been given to you during your participation in this service program.

List several specific prayer intentions for the people you serve.

How has prayer made a difference in your service ministry?

journal entry 9

after

Fast forward ten years into the future. What will you remember most about your participation in this Christian service program? What lesson learned now do you think you will still be utilizing then? How?

1990 1995 2000 2005 2010 2015 2020

According to Mother Teresa:

> "If you are preoccupied with people who are talking about the poor, you scarcely have time to talk to the poor. Some people talk about hunger, but they don't come and say, 'Mother, here are five rupees. Buy food for these people.' But they can give the most beautiful lecture on hunger . . .
>
> . . . See the difference?"

What is Mother Teresa talking about? What do her words mean to you?

____

____

____

____

____

____

Define in your own words (or give an example for):

Charity—

____

____

____

____

____

____

Advocacy—

____

____

____

____

____

____

journal entry 10

after

Trace your feelings about service from the beginning of the program to now. Do this by writing the names of three people you worked with or ministered to. For each name, write about one personal success or failure you associate with him or her.

Receive the light of Christ . . . You have been enlightened by Christ . . . You are to walk always as a child of the light . . . May you keep the light alive in your heart . . . When the Lord comes, may you go out to meet him with all the saints in the heavenly kingdom.

— Adapted from the
Rite of Baptism for Children

How are *you* the light of Christ? On the candle, print all of the ways you brought Christ to others in this service program. Print as small as you wish!

Write a letter of farewell to someone you served. If you wish, copy the letter on another piece of paper and send it to that person

peer support group questions

The following questions are to be answered briefly in the space provided and then shared with your peer support group during the assigned sessions of the service program. Do the questions as assigned by your service program director. Only one question will be used as a part of each peer support group meeting.

Session 1

Share a time that your attitude affected your performance in a positive way. Share a time your attitude affected your performance in a negative way.

Session 2

Tell about a way that you allow something you *do* to define who you are.

Session 3

Share what happened at your initial orientation and/or interview at your service site. What task were you assigned? What need does your work fill? How do you think your work will contribute to your own sense of satisfaction? Focus on feelings as well as facts.

Session 4

Share one immediate, mid-range, and long-term goal you have for your service and how you feel you are progressing in meeting each.

Session 5

At the midpoint of your service, what do you feel has been your greatest success? What is something you hope to accomplish before your time in the service program ends?

Session 6

Who is someone you admire in your field of service (either someone you are currently working with or someone you have observed in another situation)? Share a brief profile about this person.

Session 7

Write the first name of each member of your peer support group. Next to each name, write an adjective that best describes the gift you see him or her bringing to service ministry. Focus on one group member at a time.

Session 8

Discuss what aspects of your personality have had an affect (positive or negative) on your service.

Session 9

How has this service project prepared you for a life of service ministry? What is one way you could utilize what you have learned from the service program in a career you are planning for yourself?

Session 10

What are your feelings as you prepare to terminate your service at your site? Which feeling surprises you the most? Why?

sample service project ideas

There are many places and ways to volunteer, but for the purposes of listing some sample ideas the following projects have been categorized under the headings *parish, neighborhood,* and *community*. These suggestions are meant only to stir some interest or spark an idea. They may be adapted to meet your needs or ignored altogether if you already have a workable plan of your own.

The parish projects are ones that extend from existing ministries in the local faith community or that can be developed to serve the needs of the parish at-large. Neighborhood projects are those that can usually be initiated at places that already are operating in the local area where you live. Community in this sense refers to larger issues that may not be resolved, but with a small effort, the possibility of positive change is at least initiated.

Parish

Attending parish council or committee meetings. Much of the goal-setting, along with program and activity planning, takes place in meetings of chosen or appointed staff members and parishioners. Who are these people in your parish? When do they meet? What do they do? How do they listen to the concerns of the youth? **Suggestions:** Inquire about becoming an adjunct member of your parish council or another specific parish committee. Attend meetings. Summarize their minutes. Report on youth concerns. Ask for an assignment. Complete it and report on it.

Serving as a liturgical minister. Lector, altar server, usher, musician, and eucharistic minister are among the ministries connected with liturgy. **Suggestions:** Report on the requirements for these ministries. Attend a training session. Make a long-term commitment to a liturgical ministry.

Kid sitting. The typical babysitting route can take on some new and important forms. If your parish does not already sponsor a child care room for infants one to four years old, consider initiating such a place and program. Gather old toys and books. Reserve a room. Schedule two high-school students for each Sunday Mass that you will be offering the service. Also, arrange for one parent volunteer to be there too. Another form of kid sitting is to sponsor "Saturday vacations" for parents who wish to do some needed shopping or get caught up on some household chores. Don't charge for your service and see how they come! **Suggestions:** Contact the director of religious education for help in getting these plans started.

Religious education. Do you have any ideas about how to make religious education class better for younger kids? Many religious education programs would appreciate the support from high-school students in the elementary and junior high programs. Could you be a catechist's aid or start a peer ministry program with the help of the parish staff? Could you handle the social part of the program (refreshments, icebreakers, games, or activities)? Could you coordinate art projects or a sport's program? **Suggestions:** Think about what age of child you would like to work with best (preschool to junior high). Contact the parish religious education director to volunteer your service.

Helping the homebound. There are several people in a parish—usually elderly or physically disabled—who are not able to leave their homes. The parish pastoral staff can tell you who would appreciate a visit or some help with other needs. You may be called on to do grocery shopping or yard work for someone not able. You may be asked to run errands or simply share a conversation and prayer. **Suggestions:** After consulting with the pastoral staff, develop a rotating schedule with people in your group so that the homebound parishioners are visited on a regular basis.

Bereavement ministry. How can you support the family members who have experienced the death of a loved one? Many parishes have an organized bereavement ministry in which parishioners call on the family, prepare their meals, offer prayers and consolation, and represent the parish community at the wake and funeral. Are there people your own age who have experienced a loss of a close friend or family member? What are some ways that you can help them out? **Suggestions:** Contact the pastoral staff with your ideas. Listen to new ideas. Find ways to participate in this service.

Evangelization. To evangelize means "to bring the good news." For Catholics, this most often means encouraging others to celebrate with the community of faith in the sacraments, especially Sunday eucharist. Does your parish have a regular teen or young adult Mass? If so, find a way to be a regular participant in the planning and support team. Consider ways to help publicize the liturgy or to offer other support programs (socials and catechetical events) to help attract new members. **Suggestions:** Contact the religious education director, youth minister, or liturgical team with your ideas.

Dinner for the poor. This outreach is for all parishioners. Arrange to sponsor a free dinner for the poor (Thanksgiving Day or any other holiday is a good time). Invite parishioners to donate the food items for the menu. You and your group advertise and prepare the dinner, host and wait on tables, provide entertainment, arrange transportation, and take care of cleanup. You might also distribute free blankets to the poor as a part of this effort. **Suggestions:** Seek input from the social justice liaison on the pastoral staff about the possibility of organizing a holiday dinner.

Physical plant improvements. What are some maintenance tasks that you or a small group of teens might be able to supervise from start to finish? Is there a room at the parish that needs painting, a basement that needs cleaning out, a gym floor that needs waxing? What about some other aesthetic improvements? How can you help to beautify the parish grounds with plants and flowers? **Suggestions:** Approach the pastoral council or pastor with your ideas. Ask for ideas about how you can help.

Welcome ministers. "Greeters" are different than ushers. Greeters welcome people to liturgies, sponsor refreshment socials after Mass, and help to contact new members of the parish community. **Suggestions:** If you have a welcoming ministry in your parish, contact the liaison minister. If not, suggest to the pastoral council the possibility of beginning one.

Neighborhood

Recreation helper. Organized games, sports, and activities can make an afternoon at a park or school playground much more enjoyable, especially for young children. An intramural sports league, a craft course, or hobby workshop are all suitable events for a recreational area. **Suggestions:** Contact the local recreation department. Write up a proposal for a program. Make sure you tell what age children it would be for. Arrange to implement the program at a place in your area.

Senior citizen prom. You don't mean . . .? Well, yes, as a matter of fact a "senior citizen prom" might be held in your high-school gym, have a band or D.J., and plenty of decorations and refreshments. People of all ages enjoy a good dance. Just make sure the music is appropriate, invitations are sent, and transportation and facilities are arranged. **Suggestions:** Contact several senior citizen residences in your area. Present your idea to the activities coordinators. Raise money by selling tickets to sponsoring businesses. Advertise in your parish bulletin and local senior citizen periodicals. Reverse roles: use high-school students for chaperons!

After school tutoring. Sometimes all a younger child needs is someone to read to or someone to help memorize his or her multiplication tables. The attention you give to one student can really make a difference. **Suggestions:** There are many established tutoring programs. Ask your service program director to help you get in contact with one. If there are not any in your area, consider starting one. Contact an elementary teacher with the proposal. Ask if he or she can provide the classroom space for the tutoring project.

Free garage sale. You know the routine. Collect all the stuff in your house and garage that is no longer needed, advertise in the local throw-away, put the stuff on the front lawn and then sell, sell, sell! The only difference here is that you're not after the monetary angle. Rather, solicit donations of worthwhile items like clothing, furniture, household appliances, canned food, and the like. Bring them all to one place. Through local homeless agencies advertise your one day event: the "free garage sale." Depending on your attendance, put a limit on what one person can take. **Suggestions:** Schedule a facility for the one day event (a parish parking lot?) and for a collection site (your backyard?). Advertise for usable materials. If possible, arrange for an established advocacy center for the poor to co-sponsor the event with you. See if this or another agency might be able to provide room vouchers and other referral information for the people in need.

Hospital helper. Most hospitals sponsor several volunteer opportunities. You may be assigned to deliver flower arrangements or monitor visiting hours. A creative way to help is to develop and collect gift packages for patients. Depending on their ages and interests, the packages may include reading materials, puzzle books, or videos. Also, you might inquire with the counseling department to find out which patients might appreciate a personal visit. **Suggestions:** Contact the volunteer coordinator at the local hospital. If the hospital has a children's wing, you might consider preparing gift packages suitable for children of various ages.

Depression intervention. Depression, hopelessness, and drug and alcohol abuse often lead teens to thoughts of suicide. Most areas have a suicide hotline, a phone number people can call when contemplating destructive behavior. There may be a phone referral in your area specifically geared for teens who seek counsel from other teens. You would need to devote certain hours to training and answering phone calls. **Suggestions:** Ask your service program director to suggest a referral or call the business number of the local suicide prevention agency.

Public library support. A lack of public funds has forced many libraries to cut back on hours and staff. Most have many volunteer opportunities. You may be asked to shelve books, work at a resource desk, or redo bulletin board displays. With more volunteer help, many librarians would be willing to attempt more programming for everyone from young children to the elderly. What are some ideas you have? **Suggestions:** Contact your local library for volunteer opportunities.

Animal shelter. Publicly supported animal shelters often need volunteers to help with certain tasks. Most of these tasks involve cleaning and caring for the facility. If you have an interest in working with animals you may consider this type of volunteer work. **Suggestions:** Contact the local public animal shelter in your area. (If your neighborhood has a public zoo, you may wish to inquire about volunteer opportunities there.)

Museums. Museums are often in need of volunteers to help provide directions to guests, do clerical work, or help with promotion. A children's museum often sends groups to local schools to advertise its exhibits and programs. **Suggestions:** Contact the volunteer coordinator directly at the local museum.

People with special needs. There are many public and private day care facilities for people with special needs like deafness, blindness, mental retardation, or a physical handicap like paralysis. Often, volunteers are sought just to spend some one-on-one time with people in these places. You may need orientation in a special skill (for example, sign language). **Suggestions:** Many of these day care facilities are listed in the phone book under adult day care.

Community

Heal the valley, mountain, bay. What are some environmental concerns in your area? There are many agencies assigned to monitor the environment. Citizens can often participate in clean-up days or can sponsor the maintenance of areas alongside highways. They can participate in environmental workshops or help with fundraising. **Suggestions:** Look up an environmental agency in your area. Contact its representative and find out a way that you can participate.

Detention ministry. Adults or juveniles who are in jail appreciate care packages. Some suggestions are packages with toothbrushes, toothpaste, deodorant, chewing gum, and combs. **Suggestions:** Contact a correctional facility. Present your proposal. Finalize the kinds of items that are needed. Conduct a fundraiser to purchase the items. Package the items. Arrange for delivery.

World hunger crisis. Did you know that thousands of people die of starvation each day. If food and resources were more equitably distributed, everyone would have enough to eat. **Suggestions:** Organize a world hunger fast among your peers. Collect pledges in exchange for a one-day fast. Arrange for speakers to present information on world hunger. Donate your profits to a world hunger agency.

Homeless shelters. The temporary residences for people with no place else to go usually have many needs. One idea is to sponsor a series of Sunday night suppers at a homeless shelter. Vary the menu themes and make these occasions real ethnic and cultural celebrations. Plan menus and decorations for things like Italian, Mexican, Chinese, and Indian cuisines. You can even plan an all-American menu with pizza and tacos! If possible, arrange appropriate entertainment to go along with these Sunday celebrations. **Suggestions:** Contact a local homeless shelter in your area. Your service program director can help you with the arrangements.

Working for peace. Achieving peace in the world does not begin with leaders from warring nations negotiating across a table. It begins in the hearts and actions of all people, young and old. What are some peaceful resolutions to everyday problems? Think about some peaceful ways that elementary students can learn to deal with life situations other than those presented on television or in the threatening real world of violence. Prepare a peace symposium for elementary school children. It may include things like dramatic presentations of peaceful solutions to everyday problems, debates and dialogue, art projects and journal writing, and many suggestions for conflict resolution. **Suggestions:** With your service program director's help, approach an administrator at a local school or school district to propose your idea for a peace workshop. Plan a presentation for a one hour block of time. Adapt and repeat the workshop for different grades and at different schools.

Life issues. Giving voice to the right to life of all—from the unborn to the infirmed to the elderly—is a crucial service ministry. There are many right-to-life organizations dedicated to working to save lives by making these issues known and helping to improve the conditions of all human beings. Ways to participate as an advocate include being involved in a letter-writing campaign to government officials to make them aware of their constituents' opinions, peacefully demonstrating with other right-to-life advocates, and raising money through sponsors to support these issues. Direct service opportunities may include gathering and transporting school homework assignments for pregnant teens, assisting at a shelter for women, or helping to organize a blood drive for the Red Cross. **Suggestions:** Contact a local agency that sponsors a right-to-life issue of interest to you. Ask where and how you can fit in to their program.

Inter-racial harmony. Often, symbolic efforts are needed to make a point. What can you and your group do to improve inter-racial harmony? One suggestion is to arrange informal social or prayer events (volleyball games, retreats, amusement park outings) between groups of students from your school or parish and students from a school or parish with a different predominant race or ethnic makeup. Plan a shared discussion time to go along with any activity that is arranged. **Suggestions:** Talk over your ideas with your service program director or another teacher or youth leader.

Special missions. In conjunction with a group effort, it is often possible to visit deprived areas in the United States or in Mexico to help construct needed shelter for individuals and families. These programs are often sponsored on a weekly basis. **Suggestions:** Your service program director can help put you in touch with organizations like *Habitat for Humanity* or *Esperanza International* who each sponsor special missions like the one described above.

Childhood diseases. Contact an organization that helps support the fight against a childhood disease (for example, childhood diabetes). Ask how you can support their efforts either on a group or individual basis. **Suggestions:** Ask the volunteer coordinator of an agency if it is possible to organize a fundraising walk or 10 kilometer race in conjunction with your parish or school.

Alcohol and drug abuse. There are many prevention, intervention, and rehabilitation programs for drug and alcohol abuse already established. Which area of the solution do you see yourself fitting into? Could you help to educate young children of the dangers of this destructive behavior? Is there an advocacy effort (like S.A.D.D.) in your school that you might participate in? If not, could you get one started? What kind of support does the rehabilitating drug abuser need? Many groups sponsor "sober" parties and activities. How might you be involved with their efforts? **Suggestions:** Contact an established prevention, intervention, or rehabilitation program and find out how you can participate.

prayer service

"I Have Given You a Model to Follow"

The room is darkened. The participants are seated. Accompanied by an appropriate song, a candle is lit in the center of the room. After the song, a moment of silence is observed.

Welcome: You have put on Christ, in him you have been baptized. Alleluia, alleluia.

R: Alleluia, alleluia.

In the name of the Father, and of the Son, and of the Holy Spirit.

R: Amen.

Opening Prayer: Loving God,
Help us to make you known everywhere we go.
Penetrate our hearts so deeply with your life and Spirit that those who look at us see you too.
Shine through us and be so much a part of us that when people look at us they recognize your face.
Let us preach without preaching,
teach your ways without teaching
but by example.
Don't let our pride put us on a pedestal.
Keep our service humble and faithful as modeled by your Son.
We ask this in Jesus' name.

R: Amen.

First Reading: A reading from the first letter of Peter. (1 Pt 4:7-11)

The end of all things is at hand. Therefore, be serious and sober for prayers. Above all, let your love for one another be intense, because love covers a multitude of sins. Be hospitable to one another without complaining. As each one has received a gift, use it to serve one another as good stewards of God's varied grace. Whoever preaches, let it be with the words of God; whoever serves, let it be with the strength that God supplies, so that in all things God may be glorified through Jesus Christ, to whom belong glory and dominion forever and ever Amen.

The word of the Lord.

R: Thanks be to God.

Second Reading: A reading from the gospel of John. (Jn 13:4b-8; 12-15)

Jesus took a towel and tied it around his waist. Then he poured water into a basin and began to wash the disciples' feet and dry them with the towel around his waist. He came to Simon Peter, who said to him, "Master, are you going to wash my feet?" Jesus answered and said to him, "What I am doing, you do not understand now, but you will understand later." Peter said to him, "You will never wash my feet." Jesus answered him, "Unless I wash you, you will have no inheritance with me." So when he had washed their feet and put his garments back on and reclined at table again, he said to them, "Do you realize what I have done for you? You call me 'teacher' and 'master,' and rightly so, for indeed I am. If I, therefore, the master and teacher, have washed your feet, you ought to wash one another's feet. I have given you a model to follow, so that as I have done for you, you should also do."

The gospel of the Lord.

R: Praise to you, Lord Jesus Christ.

A leader conducts a shared homily based on the theme of service as expressed in the two readings. Following the homily, the group is divided into two halves for the litany of service. The leader introduces the litany. Then, each half says their portion in unison.

Litany of Service:

Leader: Jesus, model of ministry, Lord of all, help us to be people who follow in your path.

I: Teacher of disciples, instruct us in truth.

II: Teacher of disciples, break down the walls of fear and prejudice in our lives.

I: Teacher of disciples, open our eyes to your life in us.

II: Teacher of disciples, help us to recognize those in need.

I: Jesus fill us,

II: with rivers of compassion.

I: Jesus fill us,

II: with an abundance of mercy.

I: Jesus fill us,

II: with a thirst for justice.

I: Jesus fill us,

II: with light in the darkness. Lord, send us forth today

I: as witnesses of your gospel.

II: Send us forth today

I: as people of perseverance.

II: Send us forth today

I: committed to what we have promised.

Leader: Jesus, son of mercy, may our light from you and in you always burn bright as we work to establish your reign.

R: Amen.

Closing Prayer: Prayer of Peace *(attributed to St. Francis)*

All: **Lord, make me an instrument of your peace.
Where there is hatred, let me sow love;
Where there is injury, pardon;
Where there is doubt, faith;
Where there is despair, hope;
Where there is darkness, light;
Where there is sadness, joy.
O Divine Master,
grant that I may not seek so much to be consoled as to console;
To be understood as to understand;
To be loved as to love;
For it is in giving that we receive;
It is in pardoning that we are pardoned;
And it is in dying
that we are born to Eternal Life.
Amen.**

verification of service hours

Volunteer: ______________________________

Agency: ______________________________

Service Site Supervisor: ______________________________

School/Parish: ______________________________

Phone: ______________________________

Service Program Director: ______________________________

Date	Time In	Time Out	Comments/Initial

service program checklist

Check each item as they are completed:

____ Prayed and reflected on personal gifts needed for service.

____ Brainstormed possible service sites and projects with others.

____ Scheduled an interview with service site supervisor or orientation at the service site.

____ Completed an interview or orientation and scheduling of service times.

____ Consulted with service program director and finalized project plans.

____ Began journal.

____ Went to the service site for the first time.

____ Became familiarized with work expectations at the service site.

____ Established immediate, mid-range, and long-term service objectives.

____ Attended and participated in scheduled peer support group meetings.

____ Prayed regularly for own needs, needs of those in the peer support group, and needs of those at the service site.

____ Maintained up-to-date records of hours at service site.

____ Met with and was evaluated by the service program director on a regular basis.

____ Considered steps to lead from charity to advocacy in regards to this specific project and issue.

____ Participated in peer support group prayer service.

____ Informed service site supervisor and others at the service site of the impending end of the program at least one week in advance.

____ Completed journal.

____ Said a formal farewell to people at the service site and thank-you to the service site supervisor.

____ Attended and participated in final peer support group meeting.

____ Completed all necessary final evaluations.

____ Prayed in thanksgiving for successful participation in the service program.